If God Made Heaven and Earth, Then Who Created the World I Live In

by

David G. Ruiz

authorHOUSE®

AuthorHouse™
1663 Liberty Drive, Suite 200
Bloomington, IN 47403
www.authorhouse.com
Phone: 1-800-839-8640

First published by AuthorHouse   3/3/2009

ISBN: 978-1-4389-4554-5 (sc)

Printed in the United States of America
Bloomington, Indiana

This book is printed on acid-free paper.

Tribute

Bishop T. D. Jakes

How privileged I am, blessed unspeakable and highly favored of God to have such an anointed man of God, and world outreach effective gospel preacher as my Sr. Pastor at The Potter's House. Upon the sound of his prophetic voice of exaltation, I become spiritually empowered to face life's challenges through hope, trust, and faith in God. I am a new man (from disgrace to grace) because of the heart convicting, restoration, spirit-and-life Word of God that he expounds and articulates with great wisdom and power. And for this, Pastor Jakes, I honor you.

Attorney Shaun Naidoo

Thousands gather each week to experience a power-fill, spirit fix, and shekinah glory worship celebration service, and dynamic teaching of the great Bishop Jakes at The Potter's House. In such environment, it is not unusual that I meet someone as awesome as Shaun. What a friend, counselor, and confidant he has been and currently is to me. I don't know where I would be if he hadn't bailed me out in more ways than one. Thank you man.

Esteban Garcia

Precious memories. How they linger. I can't begin to imagine what great thing it is that I've done; or, could it be a trace of royalty in my bloodline that would attribute to having such an honorable, and highly respectable man in my family as my Uncle Steve. May you rest in peace. And for being a father, brother, friend, and being one whom I could rest my soul upon your heart, I stand in awe of you.

Uncle Steve (left) and David (right)

In Loving Memory

of

Uncle Steve

Acknowledgement

Florita Ruiz

Mama, from a daily force of habit, I again reached for the phone to call you. Suddenly reality struck like a ton of bricks and my soul mourned. Each break of a new day, my heart yearns to hear your voice again. I understand that the choices of a mother are never easy, especially when it comes to the well being of her child. And because you sacrificed your pride, reputation, and your very life for us—our family circle, you will forever live in your children, your grandchildren, and your great grandchildren through our memory of you. The love of a woman can be measured through acquired fascinations, but the love of a mother has an unbreakable life and death blood seal. Mother, behold your son.

Margie Woods

My friend, I am grateful to you for not only recognizing my life experience as something worth sharing with others for the purpose of ministry, but also for taking the lead and initiative to make it happen. We did it! For your writing flavor, skill, and for the many ways that you have been a blessing to my life, I thank you.

Emily Crowell

Couz', how can I say thanks for all the things that you've done for me. From your heart of gold, you have extended your love, support, advice, tolerance, and have sacrificed much in my behalf. I can't find the words to express how much I appreciate you. With deep gratitude, gracias.

Deuteromy 31:6
Be strong and of good courage, fear not, nor be afraid of them;
for the Lord thy God, He it is that doth go with thee; He will
not fail thee, nor forsake thee.

Grandma

Maria Guerra

I love you

Dedication

In Loving Memory

of

My Wife

Sheila Mayfield Ruiz

"I would die for a chance to look at you in
the face and say that I love you."

Missing you

Contents

From The Heart of David

Hey there,

Welcome to my world. Certainly my life thus far has been an interesting (roller coaster ride) adventure; and I would like to share a portion of it with you through this book for chance and hope that it will be an encouragement, and a blessing to yours. So get comfortable with your favorite beverage, and let's just hang out for a while.

Prologue

The day that I was born, I opened-up my eyes in hell. As I trace back from the beginning of the archives of my memory, like a preview of a movie, there are scene projections of a boy-child worrier in daily combat to defend and protect life and livelihood survival. I didn't have the childhood luxury of living in a gated *carnival* community that allowed children to engage in a fun, free, fantasy world. But I did live in the hood as a boy in an environment that forced me to be a man. I lived in the jungle among lions, tigers, and bears. This is the best way I can describe it in order for you to get a glimpse of how my life started. And as you read my story, you will understand the contributing factors of why I would ask—if God made heaven and earth, then who created the world I live in. It is the nature of a man to be a man—hunt, build, protect, provide, teach, lead, and at all cost—survive. I admit, I have done some things, been some places, participated in activities that were deadly; but miraculously, I lived to talk about it. My way of life caused me to be incarcerated lengthy periods throughout my life. But, man--I got to tell you--life was good for a season. I had a prosperous illegal business, material possessions, family, home-boys, women, and a loyal entourage that would carry out orders down to the very letter at my word. But when I thought I had control of my life, my way, and my destiny, I faced a judge whose warning pierced my heart like a dagger, and humbled me to a point where I began a search for the true and living God that I never knew. And now I am addicted to His Word. I breathe it, sleep it, eat it, and through the power of the Holy Spirit, I aspire to live it. This way is not always easy. But as I said earlier, I learned at an early age, to face hardship like a man. And my message to the brothers who are checking-out this Christian lifestyle is that if you have tried everything, and everything has failed, standup and be a real man--try Jesus

1

Let There Be Life

Hey man! How are you? This is my usual greeting to men and women who I know and have been blessed to see again. With a realization of how short and unpredictable life is, you just never know when the last embrace, or an *I love you* shared with significant persons in your life will actually be the last. Please don't make the mistake by the assumption that there will be numerous tomorrows to meet, share, and greet again. And man, to think that you are rich with opportunities to express heart felt sentiments to blood and heart-ties would inevitably result to be as painful as writing a check to pay for mortgage, food, utilities, and car note, and later learn that you have a negative checking account balance. Upon every contact with a friend, family, acquaintance, and even a stranger that God allows to cross your path, let there be life. Let it be a life enriching experience.

Typically when I address someone (as I did to you earlier) with a "how are you" I am really asking, "How are you doing?—or—How is life treating you?" But, another meaning that I want to entertain in these chapters is the following: How is it that you exist? And, how are you existing? What world did you come from? What world did you come to? But more importantly, what world did you create for yourself? From the beginning, God breathed life into man whom He formed (from the dust of the earth) in His image and likeness. And according to the record of Genesis, the origin of the first woman, Eve was made of God from the rib of the first man, Adam. And during the course of oceans and oceans, and generations and generations of time, the miraculous reproduction of life through man and woman continues to voluminously populate the earth.

And as it was by the power of God "The Ancient of Days" it is so even now in this twentieth century, it-so-happened (in the little cowboy town of Lubbock) a divine occurrence. In the year of nineteen hundred and sixty-seven, second month, and twenty-third day, from the bloodlines of my mother, Florita, and my father, Aldolfo Ruiz, that same life-giving breath-of-God surged the exhaling cry of a man-child. And I, David Ruiz became a living soul.

2

Man's Got To Do
What A Man's Got To Do

Los primeros treinta segundos sobre mi llegada a este
mundo, yo sólo puedo imaginarme cómo lo confundiendo
fue de oír y ver a personas alrededor de mí, y ser tocado
por la primera y unica ves. Let me repeat: The first thirty
seconds upon my arrival to this world, I can only imagine
how confusing it was to hear and see people around me,
and be touched for the very first time. But I do know that
I was born with the nature of a man--to defend, explore,
and survive. Therefore, it is fair to say that at first sight of
all of the gazing and movement around me, an assessment
took place in my tender head that triggered the activity

of my senses. With speech, knowledge, and strength limitations, I could only scream when the doctor slapped my bottom side; but no doubt, my little hands naturally took a clenched fist position while trying to detect a first opportunity for a knock-out attempt. So, the first human characteristic exposed to me was violence. It was like this: The man grabbed my head, pulled me from my familiar world of comfort and security, then lifted me by my feet for a fight. And I have been fighting since that day. But suddenly, an immediate change of emotions took place as this woman cuddled me close to her heart. And as she nursed me, and kissed me, a love connection stronger and unlike any other emotion that I had yet to experience cemented as I recognized her as my mother. And interestingly, quite a number of the fights of my lifetime have been to defend and protect her.

Why I am--how I am--who I am is due to the way-of-life values first exposed to me. Life's hard knocks, challenges, passions, tragedies, heartbreaks and troubles are the character molding ingredients that made me the man that I am. Every experience of love, pain, disappointment, uncontrollable and overwhelming hurdle I've faced in my life have been defining moments in my life. They are linked to my belief in God, my love for family, my incarcerations over the years (starting from 1986) sex, drugs, violence, abandoning my own two sons—David White and Steven David Ruiz, and a few marriages. It is interesting how one can lay the facts of his or her life on the table and review the good, bad and the ugly as I have. We all have done something, or said something that we wish we could change or erase; but, the fact is that we can't. We can only (going forward) try to restore and foster broken relationships, change destructive behaviors, discontinue to make unwise choices, and treasure family and friendships that support your well being. You can only do this through a commitment to change, love of God, and love of self, and love of family. Why we do what we do when we do it is not always easy to answer after we do it. You may want to repeat that line; and please, don't pull out your red pen. I am simply saying that when you are in a desperate situation, you make desperate choices that are based on circumstances, resources, finances, immediate need, life-threatening conditions, and (of course) measure of faith.

Hey man, what would you do if you were out of work (without a hint of landing a job in the near future) and your wife and small children were depending on you for shelter, food, and the very necessities of life? I know. It's a frightening thought—isn't it? If you have been in that situation and the action that you took is not one that you're proud of, who am I to judge you. Even when you're placed in a position to defend and protect yourself and yours against those who would dare insinuate or inflict harm, all I can say about that is this: A man's got to do what a man's got to do. But the most important thing about being a man is to be a man. Keep in mind that the big things that you do won't really matter if you neglect the small things. For example, I found some big words in the size of a book that is no bigger than the size of a book of matches. It was written by (yes, a woman) Barbara Cage. Brothers, check this out. *What It Means To Be A Man! A man is someone who realizes that strength of character is more important than being tough. He is generous, and enjoys giving as well as receiving. A man is understanding; he tries to see both sides of a situation. He is responsible; he knows what needs to be done, and he does it. He is trustworthy; his word is his honor. He loves life, nature, discovery, excitement, and so much more. He is a little boy sometimes, living in an adult body and enjoying the best of both worlds.*

Ladies, regardless of how you're now thinking of how your man measures up to these core values, keep in mind that none of us are perfect, but then neither are you. I challenge you to shift your way of thinking and consider this. Examine how you measure up to what it means to be a woman, and is it attractive enough to make a man want to be a better man.

3

King of Hearts

Don't be afraid to lay the cards on the table and analyze the hand that life has dealt to you. As you read about my life, I encourage you to study the relativity of it to your own. And I'm most certain that you'll find that my world is not much different than yours. It is only identified by a different name and involve people with different faces with a divine-driven life path of different circumstances. Key similarities to look for are the following: love, hate, addiction, strength, weakness, conviction, success, failure, anger, heart-break, violence, disappointment, joy, sorrow, and pain.

The treasure of love that is secured in my heart is stored in a deep, secret place and is eternal. It will never cease or be obliterated. In it you will find valuable and priceless gems, stones, rubies and diamonds. These are people who have made a significant impact and influence in my life. One of my most precious diamonds was born September 30, 1965, my oldest sister, Maria Veronica Ruiz (known as Betty). Typically, the younger child in the family is guided by the first born or older child, and patterns his/her life accordingly as I did with Betty. Her friends were my friends. Her habits were my habits. And her way of life was my way of life.

In 1976, Betty started getting in trouble with the law. I remember this particular year because we lived in Sherman, Texas at Westlake Village Apartments. And in this "big" city, Betty and I were exposed to marijuana and other high-ride substances. You may find it hard to believe, but at the age of nine(9), I smoked cigarettes and huffed gasoline. I remember so well Betty's friends from Piner Middle School: Pam, Belinda, and Tammy. Man! Let me explain why I remember them so well. First of all, they used to baby-set me while mama and her husband,

Jack went out. Actually, the word "baby-sit" was not appropriate in my case because I was never much of a baby. I was born a man. My first French kiss was with Belinda. And I had a crush on Tammy as well. Life, as I saw it, was good until one particular night there was a knock at the door. Of course, I opened the door and looked dead into the eyes of a police officer. And at the same time, I realized the fact that he held in his hand a shirt that belonged to Betty. I boldly said, "That is my sister's shirt." Well, mama approached the door as I spoke, and she moved me out of the way so she could talk with him. The report was that Betty allegedly broke into her friend's house, ran away, and the parent called the police. My heart ached the day when my mama, Jack, and my uncle Zeke went to visit Betty at a juvenile detention center in Brownwood, Texas. I can't find a word to express how much I missed my big sister during her years away from home. Even now, as I think about it, I get teary-eyed. It seems we both were born to lead, hustle and fight. Good, bad, right or wrong, I love my sister, Betty.

In the year of 1978, Betty came home. At this time, we had moved back to Gainesville, Texas at 202 E. Pecan Street—right across the street from Gainesville Police Department. I stuck to Betty like white on rice. I was always around her, and shadowed her every move. Betty wasn't home very long at all before she and mama fought. It seemed as if mom hated her for some reason. It could be that Betty and I were so close because she lacked a woman (mother) in her life as I did a man (father) in my life. Is my mother responsible for how my sister has struggled throughout her life? Is my dear mother responsible for the direction in which my world turns? Or, could it just simply be that my world revolves around this shining star —my mother? For certainly, it was her presence or lack of it that made the difference as night and day. Jack was a good man, but he was 29 years older than mom. It's amazing! How is it that I remember that this man in my mother's life was 53 years old when my mother married him? He had children older than her. It didn't matter, during this time when Betty was home, I hung out with her and her boyfriend. Betty's man was the son of a girlfriend of mom's whom she met at a club across the Red River. He was much older than Betty, and he had connections in the dope world. So, I'm sure it's not hard for you to figure out that Betty and I started getting high regularly. She didn't come home on time one night, so mama called the police and reported her as a runaway. Betty was still on juvenile supervision. Finally, when she arrived home, I went outside of the house to tell her that mom was mad. And as we played ball together in the front yard (remember we lived just across the street from the police station) an officer approached us as the ball we were playing with flew into the air toward him. He caught it. I assumed he was coming over just to talk with us. But he addressed my sister. "You are under arrest." And he took her away. I screamed, and shouted at him: "Let her go!" But he took her to jail anyway. I hated my mother for that. I missed my sister so very much. She was sent back to reformatory school. Somehow, she eventually ran away from there, and she ended up in El Paso, Texas with some hair stylist. I don't remember his name. But in 1980, he brought her to visit me at (my grandmother's (El Mini) house in Dimmitt, Texas where I stayed during the summer. We talked about a lot of things, but it was so painful to hear about some of the horrible things that happened to her. I missed my sister so much as I do today. After that visit, I didn't see her again until 1996 when she and her boyfriend, Cammillio came to visit me and my wife, Debbie in Lubbock, Texas. My youngest son, Steven David was two(2) years old at the time. This was the last time I saw her in the free world. My second wife, Sheila and I went to visit her on September 30 of 1998 in Marlin, Texas at the Hobby Unit. My desire and prayer is for us both to see freedom again, and take on a lifestyle that sows a harvest of the "B" attitudes. They can be found in Matthew 5:3-12.

Blessed are the poor in spirit: for theirs is the kingdom of heaven.

Blessed are they that mourn: for they shall be comforted.

Blessed are the meek: for they shall inherit the earth.

Blessed are they which do hunger and thirst after righteousness:
for they shall be filled.

Blessed are the merciful: for they shall obtain mercy.

Blessed are the pure in heart: for they shall see God.

Blessed are the peacemakers: for they shall be called the children of God.

Blessed are they which are persecuted for righteousness sake: for theirs is the kingdom of heaven.

Blessed are ye, when men shall revile you, and persecute you, and shall say all manner of evil against you falsely for my sake.
Rejoice, and be exceeding glad: for great is your reward in heaven: for so persecuted they the prophets which were before you.

I can sit with you outside of your house while the beef is smoking on the grill and talk for hours about Betty because we grew up together. I am sure I made it clear how special she is to me. But now I'm going to place this diamond back into the treasure chest and share with you another precious stone that I hold so dear. My friend, Margie asked me a question one day in a letter as we discussed through correspondence the details of my book. The question was simply this: What does love feel like? I wrote Margie back with two(2) specific experiences in my life that I had no doubt about the love I felt. I have told you already about the day when the officer took Betty away. I felt love in an absolute powerful way. But the experience was also painful. Another time I felt love most tenderly was when I came home in October of 1975 and laid eyes upon my little sister, Jackie. The newborn had just been brought home from the hospital. Jackie is the other priceless stone in my life. I consider her to be a pearl. I love you Jackie.

What is it about family ties? Is it the family ties that binds us? I consider this as something positive because as soon as you realize that someone is family, the mental "computerized' system in your brain processes this individual as a link to not only your heart, but all of the benefits that are granted as a birthright. If you are blood, you have a special seat at the table reserved for family. We automatically lookout for each other. And we possess a love—unconditional. The perfect example of a love suddenly realized is another gemstone that I am anxious to tell you about. Even though her name is Emily, she is an emerald. The dictionary describes her as brilliant. And it is certainly befitting. Emily Crowell is much more than a brilliant woman. She has a heart of gold. It's good to know that she's family. Actually, we didn't learn that we were cousins until we were adults. We just happen to meet at the funeral of my father. I could write several books about how Emily has been an anchor in my life. If it had not been for the many times that she has rescued me, no doubt, I would have drowned.

During this chapter, I have laid many cards on the table. But, the game is not over until the fat man with the Ace card lay it down. By the way, I am all muscle, non-fat. There is a quote that goes something like this: People come into your life for a reason, season, or a lifetime. It's like a revolving door. As soon as you become attached to someone you love, something happens that causes a separation—death, divorce, misunderstanding, long-distance move, custody, and/or uncontrollable life circumstances. This young lady has for sure been a gift from God. I am not sure what category in my life she will ultimately end up in, but for now, I know that she is in my life for a divine reason. I present to you my Ace of Spades, Margie Woods. With her, I call it game. The reason why is because when I couldn't be there for my Uncle Steve when he was in the hospital (pretty much on his dying bed) she was there for me. To speak to him for me, to touch him for me; to kiss him on the cheek for me, to read my final words I wrote in a letter to him for me, and to capture the love in his face for me meant so much to me. In his memory, I will share with you the letter that I wrote to him.

To My Uncle Steve Whom I love, (6-18-08). This by far is the hardest, but yet the most sincere letter that I have written, or that I will ever write again. Uncle Steve, as I was lying on my bunk on this Wednesday morning at approximately noon now. It's not morning anymore. I was just starring at the ceiling and reminiscing of some of the times that I was privileged to share with you. Oh how I miss those times, but not as much as I miss you. The last time that you and I talked, we both cried, and you assured me that you weren't dying. But we both knew different. As I was thinking of you and praying for you today, the Spirit of the Lord came upon me and unctioned me to write this letter to you. I don't know if or when it will get to you. But I just want you to know that I know that you are fighting the good fight of faith, and that you are holding on to eternal life. Although I want to see you again here on earth, I know that I may not get to, and that just breaks my soul and grieves my spirit. But I just want you to promise me that when you get to heaven that you will cheer for those of us who you left behind. Because you will be one of those witnesses that we are surrounded by—cheering us on to the finish line. I too promise you, Uncle Steve that I will lay aside every weight and the sin that does so easily beset me, and I too will run this race with patience. (Hebrews 12:1) I don't know what else to say to you my brother, friend, father, and uncle except that WE WILL DO IT AGAIN, BUT THIS TIME IN HEAVEN! Remember that you won't just walk, but you will run. I will see you again. YOU MADE IT! P.S. If I had to say anything to the onlookers, it would be this: Life is like a vapor in the wind. We are here today, but gone tomorrow. Today is the day of salvation. REPENT.

4

Matter of Life and Death

What does it say about a man who doesn't fear death? What do you live for? What would you die for? Growing up, you hear warnings and life instructions from your parents, mentors, and teachers all of the time. But it never really means much until you're faced with the hard reality of life. Choices that you make in life, even as a child will follow you throughout your life: your attitude, personality, behavior pattern, deeds, work ethics, and concern for others. For sure, certain life challenges can make or break a man. After what I have experienced in my life, I live, and exist with a sound mind only by the grace of God. As you now know, I had a lot of freedom to do what pleased me in my younger days. I loved to hang out in the community with the boys in the hood, and love on the ladies. I made myself available to everybody, and everything. I was fearless. My life choices and behavior were a result and practice of the familiar indulgence (in addition to the pain) that I experienced with Betty, my sister—no doubt about it. How can a man with my history become a committed husband, and a responsible, loving dad?

I just can't win for losing. When you follow all of the rules to be successful in life, and you carefully and proudly move into position to place that last building block on the top of the castle that you created, you exhale. There's a sigh of relief at the point when you're moments away from that great achievement. But as soon as you cement that final piece in your life that would mean a promotion and advancement, suddenly, before you can say, "Thank you Jesus" you're surrounded by a demolition army. And at the press of a button, your life has been imploded. But don't be discouraged. And don't give-up. Take the time to see what lesson can be learned from this loss. How did you fail to protect your investment? Review your blueprint, your agenda, your motive, and your layout plan. Be sure that you didn't miss a single nut and bolt that meant the security of your progress. And if you find a missing stone and it happen to be the chief corner stone, the building never had a standing chance. Let's bring it home. This is your life we're talking about. Jesus is The Chief Cornerstone. If you leave Him out of your life, how do you expect to be successful? And if you're driving down the road, and you have a blowout, and run over a cow, and crash into a tree, well—maybe God is trying to tell you to go a different way. Let Him be your compass. Many times in the bible, God changed the direction in the way his people wanted to go. Read Genesis 11:1-9. (The Living Bible, Paraphrased)

> *At that time all mankind spoke a single language. As the population grew and spread eastward, a plain was discovered in the land of Babylon, and was soon thickly populated. The people who lived there began to talk about building a great city, with a temple-tower reaching to the skies—a proud, eternal monument to themselves. "This will weld us together," they said, "and keep us from scattering all over the world." So they made great piles of hard-burned brick, and collected bitumen to use as mortar. But when God came down to see the city and the tower mankind was making, he said,*

"Look! If they are able to accomplish all this when they have just begun to exploit their linguistic and political unity; just think of what they will do later! Nothing will be unattainable for them! Come, let us go down and give them different languages, so that they won't understand each other's words!" So, in that way, God scattered them all over the earth; and that ended the building of the city. That is why the city was called Babel (meaning "confusion"), because it was there that Jehovah confused them by giving them many languages, thus widely scattering them across the face of the earth.

Even though we realize that death is inevitable, when it happens to those who are dear to us, it can also shatter your life. It was on October 10, 1993. I was incarcerated in the Cooke County Jailhouse (301 S. Chestnut Street, Gainesville, Texas). I still remember the address--ain't that crazy? I had been locked up since April 21, 1993 awaiting the Texas Department of Criminal Justice to pick me up for violating conditions of my parole. During my stay in Cooke County Jail, I became a trustee. I was a model inmate, and had a good rapport with the staff— bail bondsmen, and the judges. They acknowledged me for my bilingual abilities as well as my work ethics around the jail, both inside and out.

On this particular morning of October 10th, I was doing my daily routine as far as getting breakfast ready, pass it out, collect the trays, wash the trays, and then clean the floors and other janitorial duties. After a hard days work, I would use the privilege granted to me to call my mother almost every morning at approximately 4:30 A.M. just to tell her that I love her. I made the call, but mama took a little longer to answer this time. When she finally answered, her speech was very sluggish, and she sounded like a very old lady. We didn't talk long at all because I knew that she wasn't well. I told her that I loved her and that I would call her back later. As I was going back to my cell, I asked Officer Woody if I could call again later. He said that he didn't mind at all. As a matter of fact, he liked my habit of calling my mom every morning.

As I returned to my cell, I thought I would go to the dayroom to workout before showering. During my workout, I heard the jailer's keys at the door. This was really out of the ordinary because as a trustee, the doors to the cell and dayroom were never locked. When I looked up, I saw Officer Woody, Officer Paige, and an inmate, Rex Rainey. Rex was a man who became my friend during my stay there. He was a Rodeo Clown. The officers knew that Rex and I were close, so they figured that I would want to hear the news from him. But, no one had to say anything. As soon as I looked into their eyes, Rex said, "I got to tell you something, David." But before he could say another word, I said, "My mama's dead ain't she?" They all said that they were sorry. Then Officer Woody assured me that I would get to go to the funeral. When the word spread around the jail that my mother died, a card that Rex created was passed around for all of the inmates to sign.

The next morning, The Justice Of The Peace, Mrs. Dorothy Lewis came to officially inform me of my mother's death. She also told me that she would do whatever she could to get me to the funeral. (God's Favor!) There was no way an allowance could be possible even for my mother's funeral. But God! Hallelujah! Shoot! Before her death, I told mama that I couldn't go to her funeral because I didn't think that I would be able to handle it. Nevertheless, I was released at 12:01 A.M. on the day of the funeral, and I was ordered to be back at 6:00 P.M. that evening. My ex-wife, Debbie came down from Lubbock for support shortly after my Aunt Rose, Aunt Agness, and my Uncle Eleazar picked me up from the jail. My Stepfather, Jack paid for the funeral and buried my mother beside his mother, father and brothers in Sanger, Texas. It was a nice funeral. Mama would have been pleased.

Upon my return back to the jail, I was all right, I thought! It took a few days to absorb the reality of never seeing or hearing mama again here on earth. I eventually started to come to grip with the fact that she was gone. I would catch myself going to the phone to call her, only to be faced with the reality that she wasn't there. I can't even attempt to describe the excruciating pain from the hole in my heart. I had to find a way to soothe the hurt, and escape the memory. So I started trading cigarettes for muscle relaxers. I would save them until the weekend; then, I would take at least 14 at a time. Needless to say, I lost my position as trustee because of my consumption of narcotics, and my uncontrollable behavior. I was a total slob. The jail administrator (Mr. Brown) had to put his personal feelings aside, and place me back into a regular eight(8) man cell. Things just got worse. I started making and drinking wine. On December 27, 1993, some of the guys and myself were getting drunk. A new inmate came into our cell. The guys wanted to take his food. But I stood-up for him and told the guys that they would have to go through me. So as I was fighting one of the guys, another one would go and attack the new inmate so that I would run back and forth trying to help him. The guards finally came, and we told them that we had it under control. Well, trash-talk erupted with the officers. Now we are all fighting each other, the officers included. And when it was all said and done, one of the guys (Larry) who was there for murder, got his wrist broken by the laws, and we all got beat-down. This was on a Saturday night. The following Sunday morning, Larry and I were taken to Huntsville Diagnostic Center to be booked into the Texas Department of Criminal Justice. The situation was a total mess. Larry is still serving a thirty-five(35) year sentence for murder.

Man! When you think that you've heard it all . . . You may want to take a comfort break at this time. But when you return, I am going to share with you a tragedy that occurred in my life that was so horrific, I don't know if I will ever completely recover from the ordeal. I sometimes wonder how in the world God plans to use my tremendous life experiences for His glory. Only God knows, and only time will tell. Who knows, this book could be it. Because some of the details are too painful to revisit, I will dim the light at a certain point, and then gradually return the light at a scene where I am able to continue. If I have totally lost you, just be patient. We will connect again at the intersection a little further down the road. Kelly White (my son, David's mother) is my first love, and I hers. Debbie (my son, Steven David's mother) was my first wife. The best way to describe our marriage is that it was filled with drama, emotions, and adventure. We for sure had our highs and lows—if you know what I mean. We separated for a period, and divorced. I, again became promiscuous, returned to my familiar way of life, and indulged in worldly pleasures. In the process of a change of events in my life, Debbie and I became husband and wife again while I was incarcerated. Debbie and I survived each other for a good period. Then, off I go again into the wild blue yonder. I hooked-up with a woman who allowed me to process drugs from her trailer home. I would do drugs, and I did drugs.

This woman was as good at selling as the star Mary Kay sales consultant. But even better than her was a Black guy with whom I had a prosperous partnership--my main man. While handling my business (in and out of the house) and making runs all over the community--it was a coincidence that I ran into Sheila, the sister of an old friend of mine. Looking good—all grown up now, and has a child. We started going out. Our relationship became serious as time past. On her 30th birthday, she threw a huge hint. So, I asked her to marry me. We got married. Sheila made me feel like a man—greater than the man I knew that I was, and that I am. We moved into a trailer home in a neighborhood where we heard about break-ins and crime. Like most people, we didn't think we'd have a problem, and really didn't think much of it for a while. I can truly say that we had a good marriage. There was so much that I loved about her, especially the fact that she never fussed or nagged, even though she knew that I dipped in and out of doing drugs at times. She never had anything to say about it. I would give her the money to pay the bills, and buy whatever she wanted. Also, I had a very good relationship with her son, Hunter. Our marriage was filled with love and fun times. But if it were possible to erase time from my life, it would be the night all hell broke loose in our lives. It was a strange night, but we ignored it and enjoyed each other as usual. Further into the evening, the climate was peaceful, and each of us began to wind down and do our own thing. I was so delighted to see Sheila reading the bible.

We had problems with rats in the trailer house, so we set out traps. Hunter and I were squeamish at the very sight of one—dead or alive. A loud pop sound rang out. Snap! We caught one. Hunter and I ran to the repulsive scene in the kitchen. Hunter had a play habit of shooting trapped rats with his toy gun. And while Sheila continued to do her thing in the other room, Hunter and I had fun targeting the mouse for a shot as we pretended to take him out of his misery. We all finally settled down for the evening. I relaxed in the recliner in the living room as Sheila brushed her teeth in the bathroom. Suddenly, Sheila and I heard a noise out-side of the trailer that startled us. I thought about the reported break-ins and burglaries in the area. It was obvious that someone was up-to-no-good on our property, so I prepared for the worse. *I will have to dim the light at this point.* The darkness was as black as a million mid-nights. The darkest night of my life. The most unbelievable, the most unspeakable, the most unthinkable, the most unimaginable . . . *Now, as I shine a very soft, narrow, slowly expanding dim light on the scene, maybe you'll be able to assess the catastrophe.* "Oh my god!' After trying to comfort (4-year-old) Hunter while driving in a panic state, looking for a police for help, I try my best to pull myself together and calm down from hysteria as much as possible. The life of my wife (all of a sudden) has been blown away. My life will never be the same again. She died in my arms.

Since then, my life was threatened. Actually, I felt like I was already dead. I couldn't eat. I couldn't sleep. The only thing that I could do was barely breath. I wanted to take my own life, and attempted to do so on occasion. I didn't even feel fear when someone alluded to taking me out. I couldn't feel anything. From my marriage with Debbie came life—the life of my son. From my marriage with Sheila came death—her own death. But we will hookup again one day. (Un Rinconcito En El Cielo—A Little Corner In Heaven) Life is so unpredictable. That is why it is important to acknowledge your way to the

Lord, and let Him direct your path. For the choices you make could possibly be a matter of life and death.

Today, I realize that I am not my own. I am bought with a price. My life is not mine to take. And who am I to question what God allows. Ultimate power and control over life and death is in His hand.

Margie asked me this question once. "What would you die for?" I answered that I would die to look my wife, Sheila Mayfield Ruiz in the face and say that I love you. And above that, it would be to hear God say to me, "Well done."

5

The Potter's House

Of course I would like to make a change. Get a normal job like normal people, have a normal family like normal people, and have a normal life like normal people. But how do I get to normal from where I came? When mom was married to Jack, I would fight grown men who thought they could come up in my house and have sex with my mother—I did say "my house" even though I was just a boy. As a child, I got plenty experience fighting my way through life. I remember at the age of 12 having to fight two grown men after catching them trying to have sex with my mom while she was passed out on the couch. I can recall a time when I experienced seemingly supernatural strength from the swift-shooting rise of high degree anger like "The Hulk" and I lifted a police car. I'll have to save that story for another book. Man! Those were the days.

After loosing Sheila, I had no idea where to start to pickup the pieces of a normal life. My life with her was as close to a normal, settled life that I could ever dream of or hope for. I remember setting at her grave with a bottle of whiskey to my mouth and a gun to my head. Yes. I did. I thought about doing it right then—right there. But the hand of God over-powered my trigger finger. Have you ever tried to wrestle with God?

I began to sell and do drugs big time. You see, when I do anything, I do it big. I drove a big truck, I had a big temper, and I managed a big time drug business. When I am down--though, I go as low as low can go; but when I am up, man, I soar (as an eagle) to the highest sky. My entourage and I were busy preparing, packaging, and packing. I don't know what it is, but I have a keen sense for the feds. I warned the guys that the commuters we saw in the area were the feds. They denied it, but I was right. I can't explain it. Man, I just knew it. Trouble finds me again. My life again goes through the typical legal ritual.

You'd think that enough is enough. But, I was out and about working the business, minding my own business. I am not sure how or why the police took note of me, but apparently they were on-to-me. I had a big time dollar amount of stored drugs. I didn't know the police was on my tale—but I was leading them right to it. This particular day, I was strapped. They pulled me over. And of course, they found my piece. But even in that sinful situation, I count my blessings. It would have been worse for me if they would have followed me a little further to the house where I was cooking meth. I would have never seen the light of day again. Surely I would have received a life sentence. Trouble finds me again.

Facing the judge with my familiar face and lengthy record, I was warned of the inevitable if I didn't reverse the cycle. As a dagger, the words permeated my heart. I then realized that I seriously, urgently had to make a change in my life. I went to prison with the mind and mission to find God. I didn't exactly know where to start, so I would watch TV. There were so many preachers to choose from. I landed on Bishop Jakes while he was at the peak of the sermon. But at the time, I didn't have an ear for the yelling, so I clicked to a different channel. It must have been something that I heard him say because I ended up with Jakes again. As I listened, I was hypnotized. What a way! What a word! What a wake-up call! And, what wisdom in which God has anointed Bishop to preach. This is not a put-down to any other minister because there is a preacher for every spiritual level, and personality preference. All I know is that the gospel buffet at the Potter's House is seasoned to a taste in which I can feed on and indulge in, and is nourishment to my spiritual growth. I tried to live for God the best I knew how while incarcerated. Well, I served my seven(7) year sentence in the joint. And upon my release, I found my way to The Potter's House. I was ready to serve the Lord in the House of God. After attending for a little while, I was inspired to join the Professional Ministry Technician (PMT) ministry. For me to leave Gainesville at 4 A.M every Sunday morning to make it to church by 5 A.M., you must realize that certainly *"Something's Got*

A Hold On Me" as the song goes. And the transformation of my mind, and change of heart through the Word by the power of the Holy Spirit was the event of a new birth experience, and it has opened my eyes to a new world.

Bishop Jakes preaches with such skill and power. He expounds and explains scripture in a way that makes it come alive. I can't speak for others, but every time I hear him preach, there is a spiritual operation that takes place in my soul. The Potter's House—the ministries, the conferences, and the people—is a very important part of my life. My close friends can witness that about 98% of my material possessions consist of CDs, DVDs, books, t-shirts, backpack, Mega-fest souvenirs, and many, many of Potter's House/Jakes ministry memorabilia.

I encourage the brothers who are currently incarcerated, or have been locked-up to take advantage of the T.O.R.I program. This program is designed to help you with preparing your life for the transition process of returning to society. I graduated from the T.O.R.I. program in 2006 as well as the Prison Ministry. In February of 2007 during Criminal Justice Month, I was invited to speak to the congregation about how the Lord is changing lives through this program. It was not long after that when I was accepted into the Potter's House School of Ministry.

To me, there is no social gathering more precious than the sweet fellowship with the people of God. I believe that through the power of the Holy Spirit, the fellowship with the saints, and the anointed ministry of Bishop Jakes have filled the emptiness in my life that I was left with when Betty and Sheila were taken away from me. I am now addicted to God's Word. And it is evident that I can't live without this spiritual fix. In early 2008, I was living with my cousin Emily. I didn't have a car at the time, and a fellow PMT (Marva) would give me a ride to church most Sunday mornings for the 8 A.M. service. Since I am used to leaving for service at 4:00 A.M., I got a little anxious when Marva hadn't arrived by 5:00 A.M. So I decided to take-off for church on foot from Cedar Hill—many miles away. And it was still very dark outside. This notion wouldn't have been a problem if I was not on probation, and the Cedar Hill police didn't have 'round the clock' patrol. By the time I made a block, the police had me, and they took me with my bible to jail. Emily calls Shaun, my attorney and she pays the price to have me bailed out. Regardless of shattered dreams, my success in God through the Potter's House is being molded. Brokenness is the mark of a person who is qualified to be used by God.

David Ruiz Speaks @ The Potter's House

6

Flesh and Spiritual Warfare

Since you have so kindly invited me into your life through taking the time to read about my life, I want to be a blessing to you by sharing a word that will encourage you, and that will be food for the soul. So just hang out with me for just a little while longer.

I am a man. So, of course, I know what men want. Don't close the book ladies. I have a little "some'm--some'm" for you too. Let's just be real, brothers. The number one thing on a man's mind is sex. There may be a few "older" guys out there that may be an exception to this observation. But hear me out. It is not the only thing that is on a man's mind, but it is--absolutely first. Ladies, when you're talking to a man, whether it's casual, business, or whatever the reason may be and you make eye contact, what do you see? Do you see more than an interest of what is actually being discussed? Don't fault us for it ladies, it is just the nature of a man to be curious. It doesn't necessary mean that we're going to hit on you. It just simply means that we're curious. This is why (I believe) the toughest battle you will ever have in your Christian walk will be with the flesh. In addition, this is why when you're a baby Christian, just coming out of the world of sin, it is more important for you to attend church weekly, to indulge in the Word, and to have a routine schedule for prayer, praise and worship. Why? I'm glad you asked. When we were sinners, we spoiled the flesh. Whatever it craved, we satisfied it. We had sex whenever we wanted to, and with whomever we wanted to. Some of us didn't practice discipline in any of the areas of our life. We lied, cheated, shacked, stole, shot-up, and if it felt good— we just did it. Some of us weren't even morally good. Ask yourself a question. Is it better to be a morally good sinner than a non-morally good sinner? When you answer that question. Then answer this one. Where are the two destined according to the bible?

I beg you; if you have decided to try this thing out--this wonderful thing, the way of holiness. Just do it. Just go for it, man. I promise you that the reward is much greater than whatever it is that you've left behind. *(But as it is written, "Eye hath not seen, nor ear heard, neither have entered into the heart of man, the things which God hath prepared for them that love him." I Corinthians 2:9)*

I said earlier that I didn't fear death. But now that I have repented for my sins, and have given my life to the Lord, I am even more at peace with it because through my faith in Jesus Christ (my salvation) and His righteousness, Heaven is my eternal home. Man! You should try it. What have you got to loose. Actually, you've got everything to gain. If you fall, just get up, dust yourself off, and keep on going. I'm not going to promise you that it is going to be easy. Tell me one thing in this life that is really worth anything that comes easy. Even when it comes to women, what man really wants an easy woman? I am the kind of man who enjoys a pursuit and a challenge. An aggressive woman intimidates me. If you say that you're a Christian, then act like one. Believe me, men are familiar with the ways of worldly and street women. And when we're in church, and you come at us in a worldly fashion, we are not impressed. If we wanted a street woman, we'd go to the streets. If we wanted sex, it is for sure an easy find. But believe me, when we decide to marry, it will definitely not be with one who comes with a bag of tricks. We're looking for something special. And believe me ladies, we recognize it when we see it. There is no need for manipulation—what God has for you is-for-you.

Don't freak out if your flesh gives you the blues. Come on, get a grip when there is a tug-of-war going on between the spirit and the flesh. But whatever you do, don't justify your sin. Identify it and call it what it is—sin. Do what the bible tells you to do with it. Bring it to God in prayer. If God knew that you had the power to save and deliver yourself, there would be no need for His beloved son to go to the cross. Confess it to the Lord until one day you realize that you are completely free of that sin that had you bound. Actually, go ahead and believe it is done right now before you see the evidence. I believe we call it faith. If you're trying to give-up the cigarettes, just began to thank God for delivering you in advance. You'll see. One day you are going to wakeup and not even have a taste for one.

Be careful what you pray for. Do you think that it's wise to pray for a spouse just because you want to have sex? Well, do you? All I am going to say about that is that God knows each one of us individually and intimately. He knows you better than you know yourself. He knows your need, desire, weakness, and specifically what you and I struggle with on a daily basis. And if you've put your life in his care, just trust Him. You better believe it. Consider that if He hasn't placed that something or someone in your life (that you've been praying for) according to your clock, be careful of the temptation to take matters into your own hands. I warn you again, please be careful of the anxiety to satisfy the lust of the flesh. God always has a reason why He does what He does when He does it. You must trust Him. Trust His yes. Trust His no. Trust His wait. And as the sand in the hourglass is about to run out, and you've not heard a word, you must trust His silence. Occupy until He comes. God always has your best interest at heart. He promises in His

Word that He will not hold any good thing from us. A young lady I know desired a husband. She lived alone for years and decided to get a dog. She said that the dog was too much to handle so she gave him back to the original owner. I asked her a thought-provoking question. "If you can't handle a dog, how do you expect to handle a husband?"

7

No More Drama

It's a typical blue Monday for most of us. The rush hour morning traffic of the nine(9) to five(5) employed society has past. The children in the neighborhood have finally settled down into their first period class assigned seats from the walk, drop-off, and/or bus ride to school. And as I set along the side of the road, homeless, hungry and broke, the most interesting thing going on around me is the U.S. Postal Service, Fed-X and UPS truckers driving by and handling their business. I have nothing but time to occupy my time. From a distance, I see a skinny, mangy, nasty, stray dog headed my way. As a passing car dumps trash on the street, the dog rushes over to see if there was anything eatable in the pile. When there was no food to be had, he tramples over to the dumpster where I was hanging out, and he began to sort through it for something to fill his stomach. Most people would see such a thing and just ignore it. It's just a dog. I see it and weep. I understand because I can relate.

You have so much potential. Those words have been said to me so many times from so many different people. And more often than not those words ring in my head all of the time like an enormous church bell that is scheduled to sound every hour on the hour, and like a familiar song that plays in your mind over and over and over again. But what do I do with it? That statement puzzles me as much as the one that goes like this: **You are worth a million dollars.** Well, those kind words make me smile, but what would really make me excited is to have instructions included on how to cash it in. Maybe people are trying to tell me that I can do better, be more, and advance further in my life achievements than I have settled for or demonstrated. It is also relative to the words said to me when I've screwed up. I'm sure most of you have had it said to you before as well (if not by a parent) for sure you've heard it from your spouse or significant other. It goes like this. **You know better than that.** Even though these words are meant to encourage you, they could just as well be insulting. It just depends on your mood or simply how the receiver takes it. Consider that these words could make a person feel that he/she doesn't measure up to some high standard, or just not good enough, or not performing to the mark of an appearance of a more valuable worth. A tough guy "want-to-be" says that sticks and stones may break my bones but words never hurt. Well, I think I am a pretty tough son-of-a-gun (I had to be in order to survive) and I believe that I could handle a punch from the young Muhammed Ali better than some of the heart piercing, self esteem deflating words from someone I sincerely love. Another way I've heard people extend a bitter/sweet compliment is such as the following. **I like your sandals, but I put all of my white shoes away after Labor Day.** What a cantankerous thing to say. If you must put the but in; well, I suggest that you keep your but out. Why build-up a person with kind words, and then knock them down with a negative follow-up punch. If you've been guilty of delivering such insulting remarks by habit, just practice depositing more positive words into a person's spirit if you expect to get an incontestable return or exchange. Even if a student fails to make that top grade; or, if your spouse didn't get that job for which he/she applied, build them up with words that will motivate them to keep trying. Tell me, how do these words make you feel? **You are the best!** And one of my particular favorites is this one. **You are awesome!** How about trying this phrase for your teenagers? **You are the bomb!** If you want your spouse and children to do better in their behavior and responsibilities, say that they are already better or by faith, say that they are great. The bible teaches us to speak those things that are not as though they were. (Romans 4:17)

I don't want to fight anymore. I have decided to throw in the towel. I am getting too old to continue the chaos of anger, violence, and abuse in relationships. Life is too short, and eternity is too long. I am grateful to God for allowing me to live to warn those who walk the same dark and destructive path that I traveled to not take another day for granted. Give your life to Jesus while you have time. But don't do it because of my convincing and convicting imploration. Do it because you choose a life that is blessed, and not cursed. But again, you choose. People are more likely to be committed to a lifestyle change when it's their choice. I've decided to make Jesus my choice. No more lust. No more lies. No more drama.

Who can know the heart of a man? You may see a car traveling the wrong way; but, you don't know what's going on under the hood. We all (no doubt) have a sin that we struggle with that has to be peeled off (like the skin of an onion) in layers. So please, be patient with me. God isn't through with me yet. And if a man is to be judged by his deeds, then judge fairly. I have already confessed that I have done bad things. But hopefully the good that I have done will balance the scale. And by this, you will know my heart, and thus remember me. *It is a natural part of my life to witness to people, but especially to the brothers. And I don't know what it is, but I get a special feeling when I talk about the Lord with a family member. One day, just setting in the car with Steven, my cousin Emily's son, the perfect*

opportunity arrived to talk about Jesus, and all that He has done for mankind that we might be saved. And Emily's grandson, Little Art is so dear to my heart. He has an autism diagnosis; yet, he is very smart. All he really needs is a little extra attention. And through my love, patience and time with him, he can now pitch a ball with force and skill. When my Uncle Steve was a young boy, he was in an accident—thrown from a truck and was paralyzed. I made sure he wasn't short-changed by encouraging him to live life to the fullest even with his limitations. He lived a life that many men with complete bodily functions were amazingly envious. And no matter what went down, my Uncle Steve knew that I had his back. My heart went out to a young Black girl in a wheel chair whom I met one day. I encouraged her to not neglect to let her beauty shine. I got the message across to her that you may be confined to a wheel chair, but you are beautiful. If you let yourself go, you may miss the chance to meet someone who would love you, and willing to just roll you right into his life. All things are possible to him or her who believes.
So I submit to you, remember me by my love for God and humanity.

I am delighted that thousands of people will invite me into their mind and heart by reading this book, but my primary interest is you. I am interested in the one currently holding this book, and reading my words at this very moment. Yes, you. You have had the opportunity to put this book down after reading many times before now. And surely, if you've read up to this last chapter, then I suspect that you will continue reading until the end because you're almost there. Apparently you find what I have shared interesting, a blessing, or a help to your life. If you find my life interesting; chances are, you have lived in a world totally different from mine. I understand that to you, it is absolutely inconceivable to walk the path that I have walked, or ever considered breaking the law—even a misdemeanor. Your world consist of playing by the rules, have a supportive and functional family, have a loving and committed relationship, excellent credit, great salary and successful career, trustworthy and loyal friends, and have the lifestyle of Christian values, morals, and integrity. So to look into your telescope and view a world such as mine with a different spin, and in a different light would surely capture your attention. I would think that you couldn't help but wonder how could it be possible that I have survived as long as I have without applying to my life all that you have learned and was taught that constitute the value and worth of a man. But hear me out. Let me challenge you to think in a more spiritual and/or godly frame of mind for a second. In your world, you may be used to thinking in a worldly fashion. But consider that my worth and value apparently are on a higher scale in God's view because it is He who has invested in my well being, and showered goodness and mercy upon my life. It was His hand upon my life that caused me to walk in heavenly places, and has allowed me to set among the highest esteemed, most honorable, and elect men and women of God of our time. Yes, I have survived, but not because I have done all of the right things, and made all of the right moves. But God! To God be the glory. If by chance you have been blessed by what you have read, then I know that either you can relate to what I have shared, or you just realize that the turn-around of my life from bad to good (from darkness to light) has God written all over it. And you are excited about this great thing that God has done in my spirit. And you rejoice with the heavenly host, and saints all over the world when a lost soul surrenders to God and receives the gift of salvation. Only a true, born again Christian understands the joy, the wonder, and the miracle of such a life-changing event. You are called and have a divine charge to pray, intercede, minister, and lead lost souls to the Kingdom of God. Therefore, it's a blessing to you to see one who has gone from death to life. And certainly, it's a blessing to be a blessing. Or maybe my testimony has helped you. If this is the case, then your life challenges and struggles may be similar to mine. You are the main reason in which I wrote this book. I have a message for you. Don't loose hope, and don't let your heart be troubled. You can, and you will overcome. You may be reading this book in jail, prison cell, homeless shelter, halfway house, or maybe you're camped on the street corner. You must believe me. Hard times and trouble don't last always. All you have to do is decide to rise above your situation, and make steps toward a better life. Let the change start in your mind. See yourself with the job that you desire to have. Envision yourself living in the home that you want. Dream of having the family that you have longed for.

Begin today (this very moment) by taking control of your life. Stay focused on your goal—to be better, to do better, and change for the better. Decide today (this very moment) to let go of anger, addictions, violence, abuse, revenge, lust, lies, and deceit. God placed us on this earth that He made for us to enjoy the abundance of life. But in it, through the lust of the flesh, the lust of the eyes, and the pride of life, we went our own way and—by our actions--created a world of sin that resulted in death. Decide today to live a life of righteousness in Jesus, and no more drama.

Pray this prayer with me. God has brought me out for a reason. I survived because he has a plan for me. I release all my bad relationships, all the suicidal thoughts, the bad credit, the repossessions, the death of my loved ones, the back stabbing from my friends, the negative thoughts, and the lack of support. I made it because I am blessed! I release and let go of all past hurts, misunderstandings and grudges because I am blessed! I recognize them as the illusions they are, for God is all there is. All else is a lie!

"Now glory be to God who by His mighty power at work within us is able to do far more than we would ever dream of, infinitely beyond our highest prayers, desires, thoughts, or hopes." Ephesians 3:20

Wherever you go, and whatever you do, may an angel of light be with you.

Amen!

Notes

Printed in the United States
141354LV00001B/12/P